STUDENT RESPONSE BOOK

Making Meaning®

SECOND EDITION

DEVELOPMENTAL
STUDIES CENTER™

Developmental Studies Center wishes to thank the following authors, agents, and publishers for their permission to reprint materials included in this program. Many people went out of their way to help us secure these rights and we are very grateful for their support. Every effort has been made to trace the ownership of copyrighted material and to make full acknowledgment of its use. If errors or omissions have occurred, they will be corrected in subsequent editions, provided that notification is submitted in writing to the publisher.

Excerpts from *Life in the Rain Forests* by Lucy Baker. Copyright © 2000 by Lucy Baker. Used by permission of T&N Children's Publishing. Excerpts from *Chinese Americans (We Are America)* by Tristan Boyer Binns. Reprinted by permission of Pearson Education. Excerpts from *Big Cats* by Seymour Simon. Copyright © 1991 by Seymour Simon. Used by permission of HarperCollins Publishers. Excerpt from "The Possum" from *The Van Gogh Cafe*, by Cynthia Rylant. Copyright ©1995 by Cynthia Rylant. Reprinted by permission of Houghton Mifflin Harcourt Publishing Company. All rights reserved. "Circles" from *There Was a Place and Other Poems* by Myra Cohn Livingston. Copyright © 1988 by Myra Cohn Livingston. Used by permission of Marian Reiner. "Speech Class" from *The Place My Words Are Looking For* by Jim Daniels, copyright © 1990 by Jim Daniels. Used by permission of Jim Daniels. "October Saturday" copyright © 1990 by Bobbi Katz. Used with permission of the author. "Eraser and School Clock" from *Canto Familiar* by Gary Soto. Copyright © 1995 by Gary Soto. Reprinted by permission of Houghton Mifflin Harcourt Publishing Company. All rights reserved. "back yard" from *All the Small Poems and Fourteen More*, by Valerie Worth. Copyright © 1987 Valerie Worth. Reprinted by permission of Farrar, Straus and Giroux, LLC. Excerpt from *Richard Wright and the Library Card*, by William Miller. Copyright © 1997 William Miller. Used by permission of Lee & Low Books. Excerpt from *Wildfires* by Seymour Simon. Copyright © 1996 Seymour Simon. Used by permission of HarperCollins Publishers. Excerpt from *Earthquakes* by Seymour Simon. Copyright © 1991 Seymour Simon. Used by permission of HarperCollins Publishers. Excerpt from *Letting Swift River Go*, by Jane Yolen. Copyright © 1992 Jane Yolen. First appeared in *Letting Swift River Go*, published by Little, Brown and Co. Reprinted by permission of Curtis Brown, Ltd. Excerpt from *A River Ran Wild*, by Lynne Cherry. Copyright ©1992 Lynne Cherry. Reprinted by permission of Houghton Mifflin Harcourt Publishing Company. All rights reserved. "Mrs. Buell" from *Hey World, Here I Am!* by Jean Little. Text copyright ©1986 Jean Little. Illustrations copyright © 1989 by Susan G. Truesdell. Used by permission of HarperCollins Publishers. "Zoo" by Edward D. Hoch, originally published in *Fantastic Universe*. Copyright ©1958 by Edward D. Hoch. Reprinted by permission of the Sternig & Byrne Literary Agency. "12 seconds from death" by Paul Dowsell reproduced from *True Stories of Heroes* by permission of Usborne Publishing, 83–85 Saffron Hill, London EC1N 8RT, UK. Copyright © 2006 Usborne Publishing Ltd. "Is Dodge Ball Too Dangerous?" from timeforkids.com Sports News, May 15, 2001. Copyright © *TIME For Kids*. Used with permission from *TIME For Kids* Magazine. "Turn It Off!" from *TIME For Kids* World Report Edition, April 12, 2002. Copyright © *TIME For Kids*. Used with permission from *TIME For Kids* Magazine. "Review of *The Legend of Sleepy Hollow*," by Jennifer B. Reprinted with permission from Spaghetti® Book Club (www.spaghettibookclub.org). Copyright © 2000 Happy Medium Productions, Inc.

All articles and texts reproduced in this manual and not referenced with a credit line above were created by Developmental Studies Center.

Developmental Studies Center
2000 Embarcadero, Suite 305
Oakland, CA 94606-5300
(800) 666-7270, fax: (510) 464-3670
www.devstu.org

ISBN-13: 978-1-59892-740-5
ISBN-10: 1-59892-740-X

Printed in the United States of America

1 2 3 4 5 6 7 8 9 10 MLY 12 11 10 09 08

Student Responses

Thoughts About My Reading Life

Name:

Think of some of your favorite books. What kinds of books do you like to read? Why?

_____

_____

_____

Where is your favorite place to read?

_____

_____

_____

What does the word *reading* mean to you?

_____

_____

_____

When you don't understand something you are reading, what do you do?

_____

_____

_____

What kinds of books do you want to read this year? What topics do you want to read about?

_____

_____

_____

What expository text features do you notice? Share your thinking with your partner. Then list the features you noticed.

_____

_____

_____

_____

_____

_____

_____

_____

_____

_____

_____

_____

_____

_____

_____

_____

SAVING THE FORESTS

More and more people are becoming aware of the need to save the rain forests. Some steps have already been taken to slow the rate of destruction. Native tribes have blocked the path of bulldozers and chainsaw gangs, and many **conservation** groups have launched huge rain forest campaigns.

Much more could still be done to save the world's rain forests. Timber companies could change the way they harvest the forest to reduce the amount of damage they cause. They could also be forced to replant areas of forest that have been disturbed. Slash-and-burn farmers could be taught better ways to farm rain forest lands. By planting trees and crops together, they could preserve the fragile topsoil and use the same piece of land for many years.

Rich, industrial countries could help, too. Rain forest countries are using up their beautiful forests to pay off huge debts to western countries. If these debts were reduced, more money could be spent on developing the cleared land, and the remaining forests could be preserved.

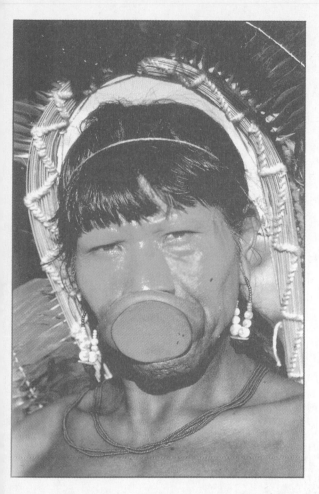

▲ Raoni is a chief of the Kayapo Indians in Brazil. He has traveled many miles (kilometers) from his rain forest home to speak about the problems his people face. Their land has been invaded by foresters and slash-and-burn farmers. The forests, which they rely upon for food and shelter, are being destroyed.

◄ Scientists believe that more than 50 wild species of insects, plants, and animals become **extinct** every day because of rain forest destruction. Many of the world's favorite animals such as tigers and orangutans are endangered because their rain forest homes are being destroyed. By protecting large areas of rain forest, these animals could be saved from extinction.

RAIN FOREST ACTION

Spread the Word
Tell your friends and relatives about the plight of the rain forests. Write to your congresspeople and ask them to help rain forest countries.

Support Rain Forest Campaigns
There are many charities and pressure groups trying to slow the rate of rain forest destruction. They need money and support to continue their work. Watch for news on television, on the radio, or in newspapers and magazines of how you can help them.

Egyptian Burial

The ancient Egyptians believed in an afterlife and that **mummification** and burial prepared the dead for this afterlife. The Egyptian kings, or **pharaohs**, built great pyramids to be their tombs when they died. The most famous pyramids are those at Giza.

When the pharaoh died, they were buried with many things believed to be needed in the afterlife. Some pharaohs were even buried with full-size ships to help them travel into the afterlife.

At the end of the Old Kingdom, more than four thousand years ago, pharaohs ceased to be buried in pyramids and began to be buried in tombs cut into the rocks in the Valley of the Kings.

The pyramids at Giza were the magnificent tombs of many early Egyptian rulers. The largest, called the Great Pyramid at Giza, is almost 500 feet tall and was built with more than two million stone blocks, each weighing two tons.

One of the most famous tombs in the Valley of the Kings is that of King Tutankhamen ("King Tut"), who became king at age nine and died at 18. The burial mask, *above*, made of solid gold, was laid over the face of his mummy. Tutankhamen's tomb also had many fine pieces of jewelry, amulets, gold statues, furniture and other artifacts.

ALL ABOUT EGYPT

Making a Mummy

Mummification was the ancient Egyptian method of preserving the dead.

First, **embalmers** cleansed and purified the body and removed the vital organs. The intestines, lungs, liver and stomach were stored in jars and buried with the deceased, while other organs (such as the brain) were simply discarded. Then the body was covered with a mineral powder which drained fluid from it, and was left on a slanted table to drain.

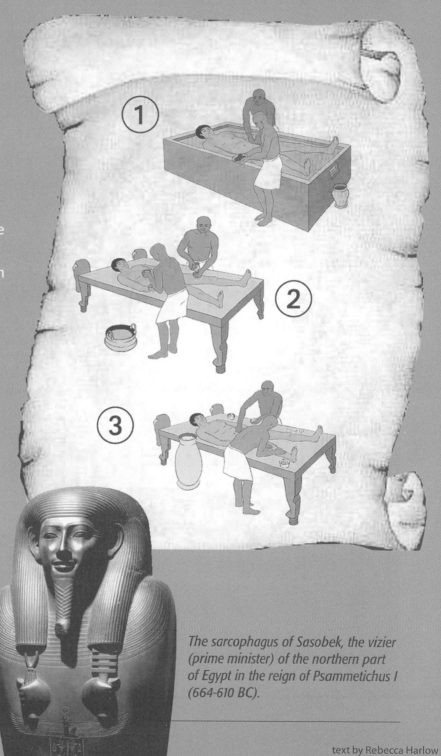

amulet

Finally the embalmed body was wrapped in several layers of bandages. Jewels and **amulets** for protection in the afterlife were placed between the layers of bandages. The most ornate mummies were those of the kings of Egypt, the **pharaohs.**

The finished mummy was buried in a **sarcophagus,** a stone coffin. If the deceased was wealthy enough or was royalty, the sarcophagus was often decorated with a painted image of him.

The sarcophagus of Sasobek, the vizier (prime minister) of the northern part of Egypt in the reign of Psammetichus I (664-610 BC).

All About Egypt

text by Rebecca Harlow

Follow That Ball!
Soccer Catching On in the U.S.

The fans turn out in thousands every weekend, piling out of minivans, sharing snacks at halftime, cheering the players as they chase the black-and-white ball around the field. **It's soccer mania out there!**

Women are winners: American women have taken to soccer in huge numbers. The surge in skills and confidence has resulted in the world's best team. In the 2004 Olympics, the U.S. women's team took the gold medal.

Soccer Continues to Grow and Grow

After a shaky start in its first hundred years, soccer in the United States has attracted more and more players each year. Other team sports, such as baseball, basketball, and volleyball, are losing players. In the twelve- to seventeen-year-old age group, one out of seven kids now plays soccer. It's an up-and-coming sport.

It's not only young people who are playing—adults are rushing to play this sport too. Over all, around 17 million people of all ages play soccer. American women especially have made the game their own. Around 39 percent of players in the U.S. are female. In 2004, the women's U.S. Olympic team won the gold medal.

Five Good Reasons

Why has interest and participation in soccer continued to grow more than other sports? There are many reasons why it is becoming popular.

▶ In football, a lineman might play a number of games in a row without even touching the ball. In a single soccer game, each player can touch the ball between twenty and thirty times—that's great for skill building.

▶ Many sports rely on brute strength. In soccer, physical size doesn't matter as much. A player's ability has more to do with skill, stamina, and balance.

▶ It's a family game. Moms, dads, brothers, and sisters can all play at their own level.

▶ You don't need a lot of expensive equipment to play soccer.

▶ If soccer is played in the true spirit of the game, few players get injured.

Soccer enthusiasts love this growing popularity of their favorite game. However, they have one complaint. Soccer gets nowhere near the media coverage of other sports, even the less popular ones. If sports channels decided to give soccer more time, who knows—in a few years it might top the list of the most played sports.

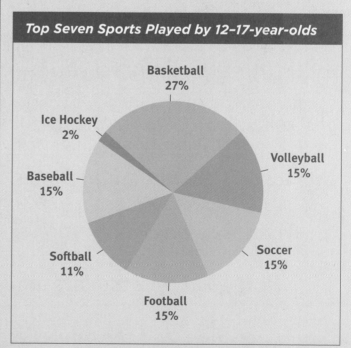

Top Seven Sports Played by 12–17-year-olds

Basketball 27%
Ice Hockey 2%
Volleyball 15%
Baseball 15%
Soccer 15%
Softball 11%
Football 15%

Source: National Sporting Goods Association, 2006

All Work and No Play
Trends in School Recess

You start school at 8:00 a.m. and the day stretches out in front of you. Your class doesn't break for lunch until 11:30, and your school has removed recess from the daily schedule—so it's math and reading for the next three-and-a-half hours.

What's so bad about recess? Isn't it good for students and teachers to take a break?

More Schools Cutting Recess

More and more schools are cutting recess time or getting rid of it altogether. Two out of every five elementary schools in the United States have now banned recess—or are thinking hard about it. Not only that: many schools are cutting back on the time spent on subjects that are not tested, such as gym, art, and music. The main reason is so that schools can spend more time teaching math and reading. Many students are not doing well in these subjects.

And even in schools that still have recess, students get less break time as they move into middle school. There are also big differences between recess times in city and rural schools.

Why Recess Works

Students have their own ideas about recess. Spending long periods of time concentrating is exhausting. They see recess as important because it's a time to:

- Have a snack and a drink
- Exercise and get rid of tension or boredom
- Catch up with their friends

Schoolwork is hard, and sitting and concentrating puts a strain on your body and your brain. Taking even a short break from

Exercise at recess increases the blood supply to the brain, allowing students to concentrate on their work.

class gives your mind a chance to recharge. Getting some exercise at recess can also help you make the chemicals your brain needs to help you store information. Research has shown that the brain needs to have a break every hour and a half to two hours to work at its best.

Also, being able to run around and blow off steam means you're less likely to fidget during class time. When you go back to lessons after recess, you can think much more clearly and concentrate well.

Recess Restrictions

Even when a school has recess, there are often so many rules that it's hard to do more than sit and talk. Schools are worried that if a student has an accident, the school will be blamed.

- Some schools have put up "No Running" signs on playgrounds.
- Tag and ball games have been banned in many schools.
- Play equipment has been removed.

Experts agree that today, when many children spend their free time in front of the TV screen or the computer, the chance to run around at recess, even for a short time, is important. It may be the only exercise a student gets all day.

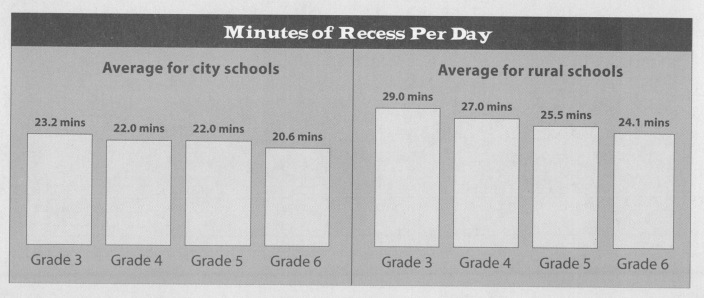

Minutes of Recess Per Day

Average for city schools

Grade 3	Grade 4	Grade 5	Grade 6
23.2 mins	22.0 mins	22.0 mins	20.6 mins

Average for rural schools

Grade 3	Grade 4	Grade 5	Grade 6
29.0 mins	27.0 mins	25.5 mins	24.1 mins

More Immigrants

In 1965, the United States government decided that 20,000 Chinese could enter the United States each year. Women came to join their husbands and sons, and entire families also **immigrated.** Many of the new immigrants had gone to college and had good jobs in China. They were looking for opportunities they didn't have at home. Other immigrants were poor and had no special skills. They thought they could live a better life in the United States.

The Chang family came to the United States in 1962 from Hong Kong. Mr. Chang had worked for the U.S. Army.

Time Line

1851	Thousands of Chinese people come to the United States during the **Gold Rush.**
1882–1943	Most Chinese not allowed to immigrate to the U.S.
1943	Only 105 Chinese people are allowed to immigrate to the U.S. each year.
1965	Immigration law changed to let 20,000 Chinese people immigrate each year.
2000	More than 41,000 Chinese people immigrate to the U.S.

They called the flight. All of a sudden I just didn't want to go! I wasn't ever going to see [my grandmother] again, and so I grabbed onto the railing and I refused to let go. I was hanging on and I ran back to my grandmother. We went on the plane and I still cried for a long time.

—Mai Lin, who came from Taiwan in 1977 when she was ten

Even though some Chinese immigrants were treated badly in the past, the Chinese phrase for "America" is *Mei Guo,* which means "beautiful country."

Think, Pair, Write
About Text Features

Name:

What information about Chinese American immigrants can you find in the text features? Share your thinking with your partner. Then write the things you found out.

_____

_____

_____

_____

_____

_____

_____

_____

_____

_____

_____

_____

_____

Index

The lion (*Panthera leo*) is sometimes called the "King of Beasts." It certainly looks the part: an adult male lion has a noble head and mane, a powerful jaw and sharp teeth, and what seems to be a dignified manner. It can weigh more than 400 pounds and be 9 to 10 feet long. But, of course, there are no "kings" among animals. The lion is no mightier or braver than any of the other big cats. It is a large and strong hunter that kills prey to get its food and survive.

Adding to the lion's "majesty," is its thunderous roar. Both males and females roar. A male lion's roar can be a way of staking out its territory and warning other lions away. Sometimes a lion will stop eating just to let loose with an earsplitting roar. A loud roar can be heard from a distance of five miles. Low roars are used by a female to call her cubs or to locate other lions. Sometimes whole groups of lions, called prides, roar together. Most of the loud group roaring takes place at night, sometimes as a response to the roars of nearby prides or solitary lions.

Most kinds of big cats are solitary—they live and hunt alone most of the time. But lions are different because they are sociable— they live in groups called "prides." A pride includes a number of lionesses and their cubs, along with several males. The members of a pride share an area together and are more or less peaceful among themselves. A pride can have as few as three or four individuals or as many as thirty-five or more. Most prides have at least twice as many females as males.

The lionesses are the core of a pride. They are usually related to each other and remain with the pride all their lives. Males stay

continues

with a pride from a few months to several years before they leave by themselves or are driven out by a rival male.

The lionesses share all the chores of the pride. They defend the pride area by driving away any strange females. One or more lionesses guard the cubs while the others are off hunting. The females even suckle each other's cubs, so that a cub may feed from three or four different lionesses to get a full meal. If a lioness dies, her cubs will stay with the pride and be fed by other females. Being a member of a pride is a great advantage for a lion's chance of survival.

While most of the other big cats live in dense forests, swamps, or tropical rain forests, lions usually live in wide-open plains. Only a few hundred years ago, lions roamed wild in parts of Asia and southeastern Europe. But today, their range is much smaller, limited to the central and southern parts of Africa and a small game reserve in India called Gir Forest.

Another advantage of living in a pride is that a group of lions hunting on an open plain is much more successful than a lion hunting alone. Several lions can bring down larger animals and kill more animals on a single hunt. In addition, a pride often eats all of a kill and does not need to guard the remains against hyenas or vultures.

Females usually do most of the hunting. Often, several females will stampede a herd and drive the prey into a trap where other females or males are lying in wait. Once a kill has been made, the stronger males and females eat first, while the cubs and weaker adults scramble for the remains. Sometimes males will share the kill first with cubs rather than with adult females. But when food is scarce, fighting for food can be fierce and some cubs may starve.

Stop and Ask Questions
About *Big Cats*

Name:

At each stop, write your questions in the box.

 1

 2

STOP **3**

Almost all the wild cats, big and small, have been relentlessly hunted and trapped by people. Throughout history, thousands upon thousands of tigers and lions have been hunted down in the name of sport. In the 1960s and 1970s, the demand for fur coats made from the skins of spotted cats led to widespread killing of the leopard, cheetah, and jaguar, along with smaller spotted cats such as the snow leopard and clouded leopard. The puma has also been trapped and poisoned for being a killer of livestock.

Though some of the big cats are now protected by laws in many countries, illegal killing still goes on. Of even more concern is that as more and more land is taken from the wild, there is less and less room for big cats to live.

What can we do to save the big cats? We can support laws to stop the sale and use of wild cat skins around the world. We can help wildlife organizations and encourage governments to set up preserves where big cats will be safe. We can learn to treasure the wildlife on our planet instead of destroying it. The future of the big cats is up to us.

Stop and Ask Questions
About *Star of Fear, Star of Hope*

Name: _____

At each stop, write your questions in the box.

 1

 2

 3

 4

Name: _____

At each stop, write your questions in the box.

 1

 2

 3

 4

And this goes on for a while until the biggest story happens. A story that will enter quietly into the walls of the cafe and become part of its magic.

For a man whose wife has died drives through Flowers, Kansas, one morning on his way to something new. He is sad. He really isn't sure where he's going.

But passing the Van Gogh Cafe, he sees the possum. He sees the possum and he sees all the hungry animals standing beneath it, eating the scraps of muffins and potatoes.

And the man sees something else there, too, something no one has seen until now. And because of what he sees, he turns his car around and drives back where he belongs, back to his farm, which he turns into a home for stray animals, animals who come to him and take away his loneliness.

Circles

I am speaking of circles.

The circle we made around the table,
our hands brushing as we passed potatoes.
The circle we made in our potatoes
to pour in gravy, whorling in its round bowl.
The circle we made every evening
finding our own place at the table
with its own napkin in its own ring.

I am speaking of circles broken.

Speech Class
for Joe

We were outcasts—
you with your stutters,
me with my slurring—
and that was plenty for a friendship.

When we left class to go to the therapist
we hoped they wouldn't laugh—
took turns reminding the teacher:
"Me and Joe have to go to shpeesh clash now,"
or "M-m-me and J-Jim ha-have to go to
s-s-speech now."

Mrs. Clark, therapist, was also god, friend, mother.
Once she took us to the zoo on a field trip:
"Aw, ya gonna go look at the monkeys?"
"Maybe they'll teach you how to talk."
We clenched teeth and went
and felt the sun and fed the animals
and we were a family of broken words.

For years we both tried so hard
and I finally learned
where to put my tongue and how to make the sounds
and graduated,
but the first time you left class without me
I felt that punch in the gut—
I felt like a deserter
and wanted you
to have my voice.

October Saturday

All the leaves have turned to cornflakes.
It looks as if some giant's baby brother
had tipped the box
and scattered them upon our lawn—
millions and millions of cornflakes—
crunching, crunching under our feet.
When the wind blows,
they rattle against each other,
nervously chattering.

We rake them into piles—
Dad and I.
Piles and piles of cornflakes!
A breakfast for a whole family of giants!
We do not talk much as we rake—
a word here—
a word there.
The leaves are never silent.

Inside the house my mother is packing
short sleeved shirts and faded bathing suits—
rubber clogs and flippers—
in a box marked SUMMER.

We are raking,
Dad and I.
Raking, raking.
The sky is blue, then orange, then gray.
My arms are tired.
I am dreaming of the box marked SUMMER.

What I Read	What I Inferred
1. "millions and millions of cornflakes—crunching, crunching, crunching under our feet. When the wind blows, they rattle against each other, nervously chattering."	The wind makes the leaves rub together, and it sounds like the leaves are talking.
2.	

Name: _____

About _____

What I Inferred

What I Read

Eraser and School Clock

My eraser
Is pink
And car-shaped.
It skids across
My math test,
Which is a mess of numbers,
All wrong, like
When I unscrewed
The back of my watch
And the workings
Fell out.
The teacher frowned
When she saw
The watch,
Its poor heart
Torn out.
Now I'm working
On my math,
And I think,
I think, I think
I know. I look
Up at the school clock
With its hammerlike tick.

I could tear
Open its back,
And perhaps
The springs and gears
Would jump
And time stop.
This test could stop,
And my friends
Freeze, pencils
In their hands,
Erasers, too.
All would freeze,
Including my teacher,
And I could blow
On the skid marks
Of my eraser.
I walk out
To the playground,
My eight fingers
And two thumbs
Wrapped around
A baseball bat.
The janitor

continues

Is frozen
To his broom,
The gardener
To his lasso of
Hose sprinkler,
And the principal
To his walkie-talkie.
I hit homer
After homer,
And they stand,
Faces frozen
And mouths open,
Their eyes maybe moving,
Maybe following
The flight
Of each sweet homer.
What a dream.
I shrug
And look around
The classroom
Of erasers and pencils,
The clock racing
My answers to the finish.

back yard

Sun in the back yard
Grows lazy,

Dozing on the porch steps
All morning,

Getting up and nosing
About corners,

Gazing into an empty
Flowerpot,

Later easing over the grass
For a nap,

Unless
Someone hangs out the wash—

Which changes
Everything to a rush and a clap

Of wet
Cloth, and fresh wind

And sun
Wide awake in the white sheets.

Double-entry Journal

About _____

What I Visualized

What I Read

Double-entry Journal

About _____

Name: _____

What I Read

What I Inferred

For the most part, they were like so many white men he had known before. They would never understand a black boy who wanted a library card, a black boy who wanted to read books even they didn't read.

Only one man seemed different from the others. Jim Falk kept to himself, and the other men ignored him, as they ignored Richard. Several times, Richard had been sent to the library to check out books for him.

One day, when the other men were out to lunch, and Jim was eating alone at his desk, Richard approached him.

"I need your help," Richard said.

"Are you in some kind of trouble?" Jim asked with a suspicious look.

"I want to read books. I want to use the library, but I can't get a card," Richard said, hoping Jim would not laugh in his face.

"What do you want to read?" Jim asked cautiously. "Novels, plays, history?"

Richard felt confused. His mind was racing so fast, he couldn't think of a single book.

Jim said nothing, but reached into his desk and brought up a worn, white card. He handed it to Richard.

"How will you use it?" Jim asked.

"I'll write a note," Richard said, "like the ones you wrote when I got books for you."

"All right," Jim said nervously. "But don't tell anyone else. I don't want to get into trouble."

Just two years after the 1988 fires, burned areas had sprouted new plants of all kinds. The pink flowers of fireweed soon appeared. Asters, lupine, and dozens of other kinds of plants grew among the burned trees. Insects returned in great numbers and began to feast on the plants. In turn, the insects became food for birds and other insect eaters. Elk and bison grazed on the plants. Chipmunks gathered seeds, and small rodents built nests in the grasses.

The young lodgepole pines are now waist high, and many different kinds of plants surround them. Before the fire, the towering older trees blocked sunlight from the forest floor, allowing only a few other species of plants to flourish there. Without periodic fires, low-growing plants that have survived in the park for thousands of years would die off completely.

In fifty to one hundred years, the lodgepoles will again be tall enough to deprive other plant species of the light they need to grow. The forest will become mostly pines. Then the fires are likely to return, and the cycle of burning and rebirth will continue.

Most earthquakes take place in Earth's crust, a five- to thirty-mile-deep layer of rocks that covers our planet. Cracks in the rocks, called faults, run through the crust. In one type of fault, called a strike-slip fault, the rocks on one side of the fault try to move past the rocks on the other side, causing energy to build up. For years, friction will hold the rocks in place. But finally, like a stretched rubber band, the rocks suddenly snap past each other. The place where this happens is called the focus of an earthquake.

From the focus, the energy of the quake speeds outward through the surrounding rocks in all directions. The shocks may last for less than a second for a small earthquake to several minutes for a major one. Weaker shocks, called aftershocks, can follow an earthquake on and off for days or weeks.

— — — — — — — — — —

Our planet's solid rocky crust floats on the mantle, a 1,800-mile-thick layer of very hot and dense rock that slowly churns around like a huge pot of boiling soup in a very slow motion. The slowly moving mantle carries along the solid crust, which is cracked like an eggshell into a number of huge pieces called plates.

The plates float slowly about on the mantle up to four inches a year. As the plates move, they run into or pull away from each other, producing enormous strains in the rocks along their edges. The United States and Canada are riding on the North American plate, which is slowly moving against the Pacific plate. The colliding plates cause most of the earthquakes along the West Coast. But earthquakes can occur anywhere there are stresses in underlying rocks.

Large areas of rain forest are sold to timber companies. They send bulldozers and chainsaw gangs into the forest to cut down the hardwood trees. The wildlife flees and, although only the oldest and largest trees are felled, over half of the forest may be damaged by the time all the work is finished.

– – – – – – – – – –

It can take less than 10 years for rain forest land to become as barren and lifeless as a desert. This is because most rain forests are found on poor clay soils. Only a thin layer of nutritious topsoil covers the forest floor, and this is anchored by giant tree trunks.

Slash-and-burn farmers clear rain forest land to grow their crops. But after only a few years, the tropical rains wash the topsoil away, and the land becomes too difficult to cultivate.

The wastelands left behind by farmers are baked by the sun and drenched by rain. The rain, which would have watered thirsty trees and plants, falls straight to the ground and runs downhill, carrying tons of soil with it. Valleys are flooded, and freshwater rivers become clogged with mud.

Tropical scientists believe that, at the present rate of destruction, there will be no rain forests left by the year 2050. If this paradise is lost, thousands of different plants and animals will disappear forever.

Double-entry Journal

About _____

My Thoughts

What I Read

COPYCATS

WHY CLONE?

Cloning is a hi-tech way to create a living thing that is an exact copy of another. Why would we want to create identical living things? For farmers, there are many reasons. Farmers already use cloning techniques to produce desired varieties of plants, such as apple trees that grow crisp, juicy fruit. One technique is to grow plants from cuttings taken from other plants. A plant that grows from a cutting is a clone because it has the same genetic makeup as the original plant.

In 1997, scientists succeeded in cloning the first mammal. Since then, debate has raged about whether it is ethical or necessary to clone animals—including humans. Although the idea is controversial, many scientists believe that cloned human beings will one day become a reality. Other technologies, such as organ transplants, once faced the same kinds of debate, and today they are widely used.

In 2006, the Food and Drug Administration (FDA) approved the eating of meat from animals that have been cloned. In 2008, the FDA approved the sale of cloned animals in supermarkets without being labeled as such.

PRO

Building a Better Breed

Since the first mammal was cloned, scientists have cloned many other creatures, including cows, cats, and fruit flies. Today, farmers pair a male animal with a female and hope that they'll get offspring with desirable traits, such as animals that have thick wool or high-quality meat. In the future, they might use cloning as a quicker way to get that same result.

Protection from Extinction

Cloning might also be a way to protect endangered species from extinction. In 2005, scientists created clones of the gray wolf, a species once hunted to near extinction. Today, gray wolves are thriving in several states, including Minnesota and Wisconsin.

Human Health

There are many potential advantages of cloning human beings. It might give infertile couples a chance to have children of their own. Additionally, people who are likely to have a child with a genetic disorder might use cloning for the chance to produce a healthy child. Cloning could also be used to create healthy organs for people who are sick.

Cloning might help us to understand how human genes work. This could lead to the discovery of treatments for genetic disorders such as cystic fibrosis. Discoveries like these have the potential to make many people's lives easier. These discoveries might even save lives.

CON

Cloning for the Wrong Reasons

Where do we draw the line between the right reasons and the wrong reasons for using cloning? If human cloning is allowed in a few specific cases, people might begin to use it in other ways. For example, cloning might be used to create children who have specialized talents—such as amazing mathematical or athletic abilities—much like animals might be cloned for specific desirable traits. From there, cloning could lead to the creation of groups of people for specific purposes, such as fighting in war. Many people argue that it is wrong to experiment with human life in this way.

Health Risks

Studying human cloning has big complications. Real human cells must be used, so if a particular experiment did not work out, the result could be a flawed copy of a human being—and that person would never have a normal life.

So far, scientists have found it difficult to produce healthy clones of mammals. For example, studies done in Japan have shown that cloned mice have poor health and die early. About a third of the cloned calves born in the United States have died young, and many of them were too large. Many cloned animals appear healthy at a young age but die suddenly. We should expect the same problems in human clones.

Even if scientists were able to produce human clones that were physically healthy, other important parts of human development might be affected. For example, a person's mood, intelligence, and sense of individuality might not develop normally.

Legal Roadblocks

In most countries, it is against the law to clone a human being, because of the many ethical and safety concerns. The United States Congress is currently considering passing a law to ban human cloning.

The Debate on Banning Junk Food Ads

Advertising Works

Food companies spend millions of dollars on TV advertising each year. The reason is simple: advertising works. It's especially effective with children. A 2006 study found that each year, children between the ages of eight and twelve see 50 hours of junk food ads on TV, and teenagers see 40 hours. About 90 percent of all food ads during children's viewing times are devoted to junk food—none are for fruit and vegetables.

What's Junk?

Junk food may taste good, but it's low in nutritional value. For example, a sugary donut doesn't have as many nutrients as an apple. Many people argue that one way to help people, especially children, to choose more nutritious foods is to regulate, or control, the messages they receive about food from advertising. Others argue that regulating advertising will simply create more problems.

Pros

Good Habits Start Young

Some countries already regulate TV advertising for junk food. England introduced the Children's Food Bill in 2006, which bans junk food advertising during children's TV shows. They say that TV advertising encourages bad eating habits among young people, because young people are more easily influenced than adults by advertising. One study found that children aged twelve and younger who watched junk food ads often asked their parents to buy the foods they had seen advertised. Young people are especially affected by junk food ads when their favorite cartoon characters, celebrities, or superheroes are telling them to buy it.

Junk food is a slang term for food with little nutritional value. It includes food that is high in fat, sugar, or salt (or all three). These foods make up a large portion of foods we see advertised on TV.

A child who develops unhealthy habits is also likely to keep on making unhealthy choices as an adult. So it makes sense to control the messages that young people receive. This gives them a better chance at having a healthy future.

Good health is a big concern to many people today. Worldwide, hundreds of millions of people have serious problems related to an unhealthy diet, such as diabetes and heart disease. A common problem in the United States is obesity. It's estimated that nearly 200 million adults and 7 million children are overweight or obese. Limiting junk food ads may be one way to help people make choices that will prevent obesity and other health problems.

"In England foods such as olive oil, honey, and cheese are labeled as junk food."

England's Children's Food Bill bans junk food ads during children's TV shows and on children's channels.

Cons

Giving Food a Bad Name

There are some big problems with creating rules about junk food advertising. For example, how do we decide exactly what is junk food and what is not? In England, foods such as olive oil, honey, and cheese have been banned from advertising during certain hours because they are labeled "junk food." These foods have nutritional value, but they are also high in fat, salt, or sugar. Calling these foods "junk food" makes it more difficult for people to understand what makes up a healthy, balanced diet.

To make things even more complicated, some ads for fast food now emphasize more nutritious choices—for example, fruit and milk with children's meals. Some promote health and fitness, too. If all fast food ads were banned from children's TV, these healthy messages would be, as well.

Some parents feel that they have the right to decide what is best for their children, and that regulating TV ads takes away that right. It is up to the parent to say "yes" or "no" when a child asks for something he or she has seen advertised on TV. What the parent says helps the child to learn about how advertising affects the people who see it.

Regulating TV ads takes away some of the information parents and children have access to. They need that information in order to make their own decisions. Making decisions is the consumer's right, not the right of the government.

All-girls' and

Better for Kids

Out in the world, males and females live, work, and interact with one another. But at an increasing number of schools, the classrooms are filled with all boys or all girls. Life isn't separated into male and female sides, so why should schools be?

TOGETHER OR APART?

Because male and female students think, learn, and behave differently from one another, it makes sense that they would do better at schools that understand these differences. Research has shown that students at all-boys' or all-girls' schools are more confident, more willing to try new things, and might even perform better academically than students at coeducational schools.

DIFFERENT BRAINS, DIFFERENT GAINS

You might not realize it, but your brain develops differently from the brain of a classmate of the opposite sex. For example, the area of a girl's brain that understands language is one of the first areas to develop. In a boy's brain, other areas develop first, such as the part that makes sense of math. Because of differences like these, males and females learn different subjects in different ways.

An all-boys' or all-girls' school can focus its instruction to meet the needs of either male or female students, not both at the same time. This helps students to make quicker, stronger progress. For example, one Michigan study compared graduates of all-boys' and all-girls' high schools with

In 1972, a new law came into effect stating that all U.S. public schools should be coeducational. However, the law was changed in 2002 to allow all-boys' and all-girls' public schools.

All-boys' Schools

graduates of coeducational schools. The researchers found that male students in all-boys' schools scored better in reading and writing than male graduates of coeducational schools. Likewise, female students in all-girls' schools scored better in math and science than did their female peers in coed classrooms.

Shy students may feel happier about participating in an all-boys' or all-girls' class. Taking part in classroom discussions helps them get more out of the lesson.

POSITIVE PROOF IN TEST RESULTS

In 2000, the principal of Thurgood Marshall Elementary School in Seattle, Washington, decided to separate the students at his school into all-boys' or all-girls' classrooms. He hoped that this would improve the behavior of students. Not only did behavior improve, but academic results did, too. Boys increased their average scores in reading from about 20 percent to 66 percent. In writing, they scored the highest in their state. An inner-city high school in Montreal, Canada, also made the switch from coed to all-boys' and all-girls' classrooms in 2000. Before then, an average of only about 65 percent of students would pass final exams each year. Since the switch, the average has soared to 80 percent.

BUILDING CONFIDENCE

Supporters of all-boys' and all-girls' classrooms argue that in those environments, the students are less distracted. This makes it easier for all students to focus on the lesson.

Students who feel shy around people of the opposite sex could benefit the most from all-boys' or all-girls' schools. Without the pressure of worrying about how they might look to members of the opposite sex, they can feel free to be themselves. For example, they might explore subjects they wouldn't normally explore and join clubs or sports teams. Shy students are more likely to feel more comfortable in an all-boys' or all-girls' class, so they're more likely to feel enthusiastic about speaking up in class, asking questions, and joining in class discussions.

Many people argue that an all-boys' or all-girls' education could make it more difficult for young people to learn how to relate to members of the opposite sex. It's true that we live in a world where males and females live and work with one another, not segregated as in boys' or girls' schools. But many graduates of these schools say that they feel confident not only about their academic abilities, but they're also more confident in their personalities. And this confidence can give graduates a head start in building friendships with the opposite sex.

AN INCREASINGLY POPULAR OPTION

All-boys' and all-girls' classes and schools are gaining favor across the United States. In 1995, only three public schools in the United States offered this option. Today, there are more than 250. School districts, parents, and students are increasingly getting on board with all-boys' and all-girls' education as a great way to boost students' scores and confidence.

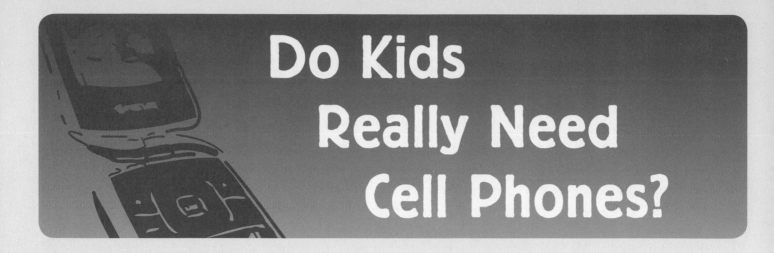

Do Kids Really Need Cell Phones?

Benefits Beyond the Cool Factor

There are more than 2 billion cell phone users worldwide—and the trend is catching on among eight- to twelve-year-olds. With bright colors and catchy ringtones, cell phones are hard for young people to resist.

But why does a person as young as eight years old need a cell phone? He or she is likely to come up with a list of reasons why, including, "All my friends have them." However, for very young kids, there are many benefits to having cell phones, beyond the obvious "cool" factor.

A Cell Phone Is a Lifeline

In an emergency, a cell phone can be a lifeline. Cell phones allow children to dial 911 or call their parents if there is an accident or emergency. Cell phones allow children to stay in contact with family. Children, parents, and other caregivers are often in different places throughout the day, and things often don't go as expected. For example, if soccer practice ends early or a parent is stuck in traffic, a cell phone can let everyone know how plans have changed.

As our lives become busier, the number of students at home alone after school is increasing. Between 1970 and 2002, the number of children in the United States with mothers in the labor force increased from about 39 percent to 63 percent. Today, about 40 percent of twelve-year-old students are alone at home after school.* This means that it is more important than ever to have a way of keeping in touch with family—and a way of getting help in an emergency.

*Source: U.S. Dept. of Commerce, U.S. Census Bureau, 2002.

Cell phones can help the day run smoothly by keeping family members in touch with one another.

Easy to Set Controls and Limits

Many people worry that cell phones put young children in danger. Bullies or even criminals might use the phones to contact children, and the Internet features of cell phones put children even more at risk. There is also the chance that children can run up high cell phone charges.

However, many cell phones now have parental controls. For example, it's possible to place limits on who can call and be called with some phones. Many cell phones don't have Internet access or text messaging. Some have Global Positioning System (GPS) tracking so that parents can find their child easily, using another cell phone or a website.

Parents can also opt for a prepaid plan so that their child can't go over spending limits. So, it's possible for children to get the benefits of cell phone use without the risks.

Workplaces around the world are becoming more and more reliant on technology.

Preparing for Working with Technology

In the near future, many jobs will be dependent on cell phones and similar devices. Many people predict that mobile devices such as cell phones will be as important in the future as the computer has been in the last twenty years. One way to ensure that young people are familiar with this technology is to allow them to use cell phones now.

Using a cell phone isn't limited to text messaging and talking any more. For example, cell phones can be helpful when doing schoolwork. On a standard cell phone, students can check the Internet for definitions and spellings of tricky words, take photos and make short videos for school projects, and listen to audio books using an MP3 player. Carrying out a variety of tasks using cell phones can help boost young people's confidence around technology—and, in turn, help them feel confident when they grow up and begin working.

Cell Phones Teach Responsibility

Owning a tool such as a cell phone can be a great way for a child to learn responsibility. Because cell phones are valuable and can be used in different ways, children must learn to use them wisely—for example, making sure they don't lose them, keeping them charged, and using them only when they are not in school. These things help young people learn to treat personal possessions with care. Learning responsibility in this way helps children to respect other people's belongings, too.

An Unstoppable Trend

Researchers say that about 6 million of the 20 million American children between eight and twelve years old had cell phones by the end of 2006. Researchers also predict that, by 2010, there will be 10.5 million preteen cell phone users. If young children don't already own cell phones, it's likely that they will in the future. The best way for young people to benefit from this technology is to learn to use it responsibly today.

How to Make an Origami Cup

Now you can learn to make a handy cup using only a sheet of paper!
Begin with a square piece of paper and follow the instructions below:

Step 1:

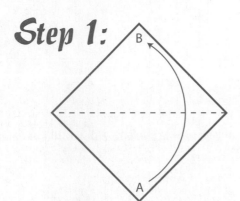

Fold your square on the diagonal,
matching up corners **A** and **B**.

Step 2:

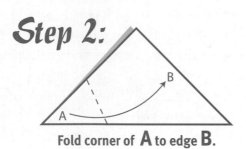

Fold corner of **A** to edge **B**.

Step 3:

Fold corner of **A** to corner **B**.

Step 4:

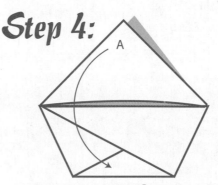

Take the top flap (flap **A**) and fold down
toward you. Turn the cup over and repeat
the step with the other remaining flap.

Step 5:

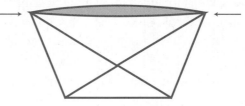

Gently push sides in to form your cup.
If you followed the instructions above, your cup
should look like this and be able to hold water.
Enjoy your cup!

Ashton Hammerheads Schedule
for July, 2008

Sunday	Monday	Tuesday	Wednesday	Thursday	Friday	Saturday
		1 vs Glen Hill @ Bank Park	**2** vs Flourbell @ Fair Stad 12:30 p.m.	**3**	**4** vs Ardmore	**5** vs Plymouth 12:15 p.m.
6 vs Plymouth	**7** vs Paulsboro	**8** vs Paulsboro	**9** vs Paulsboro 12:30 p.m.	**10**	**11** vs Mt Holly @ Holly Stad 9:00 p.m.	**12** vs Mt Holly @ Holly Stad
13 vs Mt Holly @ Holly Stad 3:00 p.m.	**14** vs Beverley @ Bev Stad 9:00 p.m.	**15** vs Beverley @ Bev Stad 9:00 p.m.	**16** vs Springfield @ Spring Bank 1:30 p.m.	**17**	**18** vs Bridgeport @ Broomall	**19** vs Bridgeport @ Broomall 2:30 p.m.
20 vs Ridley Crew @ Broomall 1:30 p.m.	**21**	**22** vs Wishton	**23** vs Wishton	**24** vs Oreland 12:15 p.m.	**25** vs Oreland 9:00 p.m.	**26** vs Chester
27 vs Chester 1:15 p.m.	**28** vs Glenolden @ Wales Park	**29** vs Paulsboro @ Wales Park 2:00 p.m.	**30** vs Paulsboro @ Wales Park	**31** vs Paulsboro @ Wales Park		

Hammerheads t-shirt day
(free t-shirt for first 1500 fans)

Hammerheads cap day
(free baseball cap for all fans under fifteen)

League Championship ticket raffle
(all fans entered into a drawing for 4 free tickets to the League Championship game)

☐ = Hammerheads Home Game   ▨ = Hammerheads Away Game

All games begin at 6:00 p.m. unless otherwise indicated.

Tickets $25

FRONTIER FUN PARK

Home of the Legendary PINE MOUNTAIN

At 460 feet, Pine Mountain is the nation's highest roller coaster!
We think it's the world's greatest, most thrilling roller coaster ever!
You must be more than 4 feet tall to ride the Pine Mountain.

SINGLE-DAY PASSES

	Adults (Age 10+)	Children (Ages 3–9)
1-DAY BASIC PASS	**$40.00**	**$30.00**

Includes entry to all main attractions (does not include Pine Mountain roller coaster)

	Adults (Age 10+)	Children (Ages 3–9)
1-DAY PINE MOUNTAIN PASS	**$50.00**	**$40.00**

Includes entry to all main attractions, including Pine Mountain roller coaster

1-DAY PINE MOUNTAIN FAMILY PASS   **$140.00**

(Up to 2 adults and 2 children aged 3–9)
Includes entry to all main attractions, including Pine Mountain roller coaster

1-DAY PINE MOUNTAIN PLUS FAMILY PASS   **$160.00**

(Up to 2 adults and 2 children aged 3–9)
Includes entry to all main attractions, including Pine Mountain roller coaster, plus a 20% discount on all purchases from the Frontier Cabin Outdoor Superstore

ONE-WEEK PASSES

1-WEEK PINE MOUNTAIN FAMILY PASS   **$320.00**

(Up to 2 adults and 2 children aged 3–9)
Includes entry to all main attractions, including Pine Mountain roller coaster, for 7 consecutive days

Disclaimer
The safety of our guests is Frontier Fun Park's highest priority. However, the Frontier Fun Park will not be liable for any injuries, damages, or losses that occur in connection with the Fun Park's activities.

— CONTENTS —

1. Broken Promises

THE TRAIL OF TEARS

In the 1800s, European settlers flooded into the United States. As they began building new lives for themselves—mining for gold and building towns, farms, canals, and railroads—they took over more and more land.

In 1836, the U.S. government tried to resolve its "Indian problem" by giving the eastern Native American tribes two years to move westward from their homelands. If these tribes didn't move within the two-year period, they would be forced to leave. While many tribes had little choice but to go, some tribes fought against removal.

For example, only 2,000 of the 18,000 Native Americans in the area known today as Georgia had moved by the end of the two years. In 1838, government soldiers force-marched the Cherokee and other tribes from Georgia all the

Painting by Robert Lindneux, Woolaroc Museum, Bartlesville, Oklahoma

"It is with sorrow we are forced by the white man to quit the scenes of our childhood. We bid farewell to it and all we hold dear."

—Charles Hicks, Cherokee chief

1. Broken Promises

way to present-day Oklahoma. During the long, difficult journey of more than 1,000 miles, about 4,000 people became ill and died. This journey became known as the Trail of Tears.

Present-day Oklahoma was set aside as Native American territory. However, this land was different from the land the eastern tribes were used to. The crops they had grown in the East didn't grow on the new land, there were few wild animals to hunt, and the plants and geography were unfamiliar. The Native Americans had no way to rebuild the life they had built for themselves in the East. Even as the tribes struggled to survive in Oklahoma, much of the land they had been given was taken back by the U.S. government as the population of white settlers grew.

THE RESERVATIONS

The plains (or western) tribes were also struggling to survive. When gold was discovered in California in 1849, a flood of white settlers began traveling west hoping to make their fortunes, passing through Native American hunting grounds on the way. Tensions began to build as the two peoples crossed paths.

Unlike Native Americans, the settlers were not respectful of the land. They cut down many trees and hunted too many animals. There were so many violent **confrontations** between Native Americans and settlers that the U.S. government became worried that there might be a full-scale war.

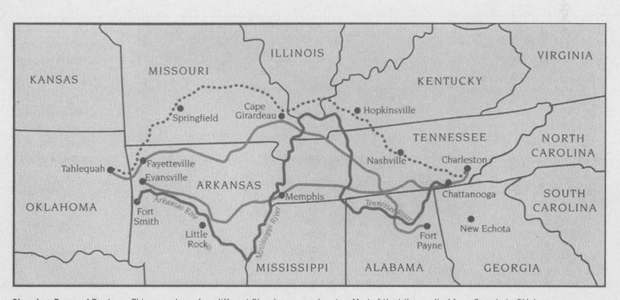

Cherokee Removal Routes   This map shows four different Cherokee removal routes. Most of the tribes walked from Georgia to Oklahoma. Some traveled by a combination of wagon, boat, and horse.

2. Lost Land, Lost Independence

WARDS OF THE STATE

In 1871, all Native American tribes lost their right to sign treaties when the U.S. government declared that it no longer recognized the tribes as nations, but instead thought of Native Americans as "wards of the state." A ward of the state is a person who cannot take responsibility for himself or herself, such as a young child.

U.S. troops and government agents took control of the reservations. The agents distributed rations of food and secondhand clothes. The Native Americans were treated as if they could not care for themselves, and on the reservations, this became true. The Native Americans were forced to depend on the government because they no longer had the resources they needed to make a living. They were a long way from the land they knew.

The reservations were on land that none of the settlers wanted. Many of the tribes had never learned to farm in the European American way, and the poor-quality soil on the reservations made it impossible to learn. So many bison had been killed to make way for the building of the railroad that there were not enough bison to hunt. The tribes could not feed themselves or their families.

Now the United States had a different kind of "Indian problem." Native Americans were no longer **self-sufficient**. If they were not able to provide for themselves on the reservations, their children would not learn how to provide for themselves, either.

Marjorie C. Leggitt

1. Broken Promises

way to present-day Oklahoma. During the long, difficult journey of more than 1,000 miles, about 4,000 people became ill and died. This journey became known as the Trail of Tears.

Present-day Oklahoma was set aside as Native American territory. However, this land was different from the land the eastern tribes were used to. The crops they had grown in the East didn't grow on the new land, there were few wild animals to hunt, and the plants and geography were unfamiliar. The Native Americans had no way to rebuild the life they had built for themselves in the East. Even as the tribes struggled to survive in Oklahoma, much of the land they had been given was taken back by the U.S. government as the population of white settlers grew.

THE RESERVATIONS

The plains (or western) tribes were also struggling to survive. When gold was discovered in California in 1849, a flood of white settlers began traveling west hoping to make their fortunes, passing through Native American hunting grounds on the way. Tensions began to build as the two peoples crossed paths.

Unlike Native Americans, the settlers were not respectful of the land. They cut down many trees and hunted too many animals. There were so many violent **confrontations** between Native Americans and settlers that the U.S. government became worried that there might be a full-scale war.

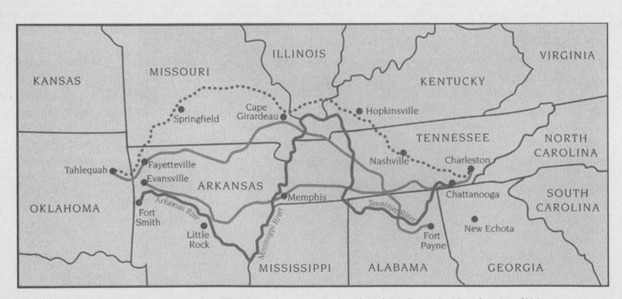

Cherokee Removal Routes   This map shows four different Cherokee removal routes. Most of the tribes walked from Georgia to Oklahoma. Some traveled by a combination of wagon, boat, and horse.

Engraving. Kansas State Historical Society

Native Americans fought hard to combat the sudden flood of settlers into their homelands.

In 1851, in an attempt to keep the Native Americans out of the settlers' way, the U.S. Congress introduced the Indian **Appropriation** Act. The act said the Lakota, Cheyenne, Arapaho, Crow, and other western tribes would live on areas of land known as reservations until they stopped attacking the settlers. Each tribe was given a specific piece of land. The U.S. government agreed that the tribes would receive a yearly payment for as long as they lived on the reservations, but soon the U.S. government reduced the number of years for payment. In some cases, the U.S. government had promised the same land to more than one tribe, and fights broke out between the tribes as they competed for water, game, and land. As more and more settlers moved westward in search of gold and land, the government also made the reservations smaller.

4. Boarding School Life

THE JOURNEY

In October 1879, 82 boys and girls began their journey from South Dakota to Carlisle Indian Industrial School. When they boarded the train, they were told that they were "going to school." They didn't know why they were taken from their homes, how far they would travel, or whether they would see their families again. One boy, named Ota Kte, thought that they were going to be killed. However, believing that he was doing something brave for his tribe, Ota Kte boarded the train with the others.

The long, noisy train ride was the first of many strange experiences for the children. Whenever the train stopped in a city, crowds of people stared at them, curious to see the "wild" children. The children huddled inside, frightened and confused.

"BEFORE" AND "AFTER"

When the hungry, exhausted children arrived at Carlisle, Captain Pratt's program began immediately. First, the children were photographed. Next, they were stripped of their traditional clothing, including the special beaded necklaces their parents had given them to mark an important journey or change in their lives. Everything was placed in a pile and burned. The children were then scrubbed in hot baths and given uniforms to wear. The children were used to wearing loose clothing and soft moccasins on their feet, so the stiff collars, belts, and boots made them feel trapped and **anxious**. They felt as if they were locked in cages.

Captain Pratt also thought that the boys' long hair made them look like savages and had it cut short. Traditionally, the only time Native Americans cut their hair was during times of **mourning**. The children wailed as it was cut.

Finally, with their new clothes and short hair, the children were photographed again.

NEW NAMES

At the school, the children were **immersed** in English. Immersion is a way of teaching foreign languages in which teachers and students use only the foreign language. The children were forbidden to speak their native languages at any time. They had no way to express their feelings of homesickness and confusion because they didn't know the English words for their thoughts and feelings. If Native American

Marjorie C. Leggitt

Pratt wanted to show "before" and "after" photographs to people so that he could prove that he had "civilized" the children.

4. Boarding School Life

BOARDING SCHOOL LIFE

What's in a Name?

Native American names are given to honor what a person has done or what qualities he or she has. For example, the Cherokee name *Ayita* means "first to dance" and the Sioux name *Hantaywee* means "faithful." *Ota Kte*, meaning "plenty kill," had been given his name to honor his father's skills as a warrior.

children spoke their native languages at school, they were made to wash their own mouths with soap.

As part of their English language immersion, the children chose English names for themselves from a list on a chalkboard. The names belonged to U.S. presidents and other important people, but the scribbles on the chalkboard meant nothing to the children. With new names and appearances, the children no longer felt like themselves.

UNFAMILIAR ROUTINES

At mealtimes, the children had to march like soldiers to long dining tables. They waited for a bell to ring before sitting down to eat. The children had never sat at tables or used knives, forks, and napkins before. Most had never eaten such foods as flour or sugar.

The children became sick because of their new diet and because they were living in such close quarters. Diseases then spread quickly in the crowded, drafty **dormitories**. The children had no **immunity** against illnesses such as measles, mumps, and influenza. In the first year, 6 boys died and 15 children were sent home ill.

As bad as the days were, the nights were worse. As one Sioux woman, Zitkala-Sa, later wrote, "Not a soul came to comfort me. I was only one of many little animals driven by a herder." The dormitories were very strange to the children. At home, there was no furniture, and families slept together in round **tepees** and lodges, but at Carlisle, beds were arranged in long rows, and the children were forbidden to speak to one another.

Marjorie C. Leggitt

6. Boarding Schools in Question

A GOOD INVESTMENT?

The Carlisle school opened in 1879. Initially, the U.S. government saw Carlisle as a great success. Other boarding schools for Native American children began to open. By 1902, there were 25 boarding schools in 15 states, and very few Native American students were left attending day schools on the reservations. Almost 10,000 children were enrolled in boarding schools.

However, despite the $45 million spent between 1880 and 1900 to "educate" about 20,000 Native American children in the ways of European American society, very few students actually graduated from the schools. For example, only 8 percent of the students who attended Carlisle ever graduated. Many students ran away, and many of those who remained were not educated—or Americanized—in the way supporters of the schools had hoped. Some people in the U.S. government began to question how well the schools really worked.

THE MERIAM REPORT

In 1928, the U.S. government could see that many of its Native American policies had failed. A researcher named Lewis Meriam was sent to prepare a report about the conditions on Native American reservations and in boarding schools. Meriam led a team of experts, including scientists, historians, teachers, and lawyers. They found that in all areas of life, Native Americans were suffering—especially children in boarding schools. Just a few of the findings in Meriam's report, called "The Problem of Indian Administration," were:

- Health conditions in boarding schools were terrible.

- A diet lacking in nutrients was causing children to become ill.

- Schools considered work such as farming and cleaning to be more important than classroom education.

- Schools followed **rigid** routines that stopped children from being creative.

- Lessons should include Native American subjects to help students feel more comfortable in unfamiliar classrooms.

CLOSED FOR GOOD

At the time of the Meriam Report, almost 80 percent of Native American school-aged children were in boarding schools. The report was embarrassing for the U.S. government because it showed that children should not be taken away from their homes to be educated.

LS IN QUESTION

The strict routines and teaching style of boarding schools had done little to help Native American students learn. This photograph shows students during a mathematics class at Carlisle.

Meriam and his team concluded that Native American children should instead attend day schools or public schools that would keep them connected to their families and communities. By the 1930s, most of the boarding schools, including Carlisle, had been closed for good.

Double-entry Journal
About *Survival and Loss:*
Native American Boarding Schools

Examples from the text

Relationships

Chronological

Cause and Effect

Compare and Contrast

> **What is important to know or remember in the story? Share your thinking with your partner. Then write your ideas below.**

_____

_____

_____

_____

_____

_____

_____

_____

_____

_____

_____

_____

_____

_____

_____

_____

But then everything began to change.
The men went to the Grange Hall
time after time after time. The women, too.
Only nobody asked us kids.
They all listened to men from Boston
because the city of Boston, sixty miles away,
needed lots of water.
Boston had what Papa called
"a mighty long thirst,"
and no water to quench it.
We had water here in the valley:
good water, clear water,
clean water, cold water,
running between the low hills.
We could trade water for money,
or water for new houses,
or water for a better life.
So it was voted in Boston to drown our towns
that the people in the city might drink.

Think, Pair, Write
About *A River Ran Wild*

Name: _____

> **What is important to know or remember in the story? Share your thinking with your partner. Then write your ideas below.**

_____

_____

_____

_____

_____

_____

_____

_____

_____

_____

_____

_____

_____

_____

_____

_____

At the start of the new century, an industrial revolution came to the Nashua's banks and waters. Many new machines were invented. Some spun thread from wool and cotton. Others wove the thread into cloth. Some machines turned wood to pulp, and others made the pulp into paper. Leftover pulp and dye and fiber was dumped into the Nashua River, whose swiftly flowing current washed away the waste.

These were times of much excitement, times of "progress" and "invention." Factories along the Nashua River made new things of new materials. Telephones and radios and other things were made of plastics. Chemicals and plastic waste were also dumped into the river. Soon the Nashua's fish and wildlife grew sick from this pollution.

The paper mills continued to pollute the Nashua's waters. Every day for many decades pulp was dumped into the Nashua, and as the pulp clogged up the river, it began to run more slowly.

As the pulp decomposed, bad smells welled up from the river. People who lived near the river smelled its stench and stayed far from it. Each day as the mills dyed paper red, green, blue, and yellow, the Nashua ran whatever color the paper was dyed.

Soon no fish lived in the river. No birds stopped on their migration. No one could see pebbles shining up through murky water. The Nashua was dark and dirty. The Nashua was slowly dying.

Summary

A River Ran Wild by Lynne Cherry

This book tells the story of the Nashua River, a river that ran wild through forests filled with animals. A group of native people settled near the river and named it Nash-a-way, which means River with the Pebbled Bottom. These people lived in peace until white settlers arrived and began taking more of the land for themselves. The two groups fought and the native people were driven from the land.

Over the years, factories were built that polluted the river, killing the animals and turning the water murky and smelly. After years of neglect, two people decided to do something to save the Nashua River. Their efforts led to the passing of new laws that stopped factories from polluting the river. Slowly the Nashua's current cleaned the river, and once again, a river runs wild.

This is the true story of how the towns in the Swift River Valley in Massachusetts were drowned to create the Quabbin Reservoir. The narrator begins by describing how her world felt like a safe place as a child growing up in the valley. Then life changed when men from Boston, a city with "a mighty long thirst" and not enough water, came to buy the land to build a reservoir. Graves were moved, trees and houses were destroyed, and families moved away. The rivers were dammed, and slowly, over seven long years, the valley filled with water.

Years later, as an adult, the narrator rows out onto the reservoir with her father and remembers her life as a child in the Swift River Valley.

For years and years, for what seems like forever, I've gone to BUELLS when I had a dime to spare. It's a run-down, not very clean corner store. Kids go there mostly, for licorice and bubble gum and jawbreakers and Popsicles and comic books and cones. She only has three flavors and the cones taste stale. Still, she'll sell you one scoop for fifteen cents. It's not a full scoop but it's cheaper than anywhere else. It's the only place I know where a kid can spend one penny.

Mrs. Buell is run-down too, and a grouch. She never smiles or asks you how you are. Little kids are scared to go in there alone. We laugh at them but really, we understand. We felt it too, when we were smaller and had to face her towering behind the counter.

– – – – – – – – –

She was always the same except that once. I tripped going in, and fell and scraped my knee. It hurt so much that I couldn't move for a second. I was winded too, and I had to gasp for breath. I managed not to cry out but I couldn't keep back the tears.

Mrs. Buell is big but she moved like lightning. She hauled a battered wooden chair out from behind the curtain that hung across the back. Then, without a word, she picked me up and sat me down on it. We were alone in the store but I wasn't afraid. Her hands, scooping me up, had been work-roughened; hard but kind.

She still didn't speak. Instead, she took a bit of rag out of her sweater pocket, bent down and wiped the smear of blood off my knee. The rag looked grayish but her hands were gentle. I think she liked doing it. Then she fetched a Band-Aid and stuck it on.

continues

"Does it still sting?" she asked, speaking at last, in a voice I'd never heard her use before.

— — — — — — — — —

I shook my head. And she smiled. At least I think she did. It only lasted a fraction of a second. And I wasn't looking straight at her.

At that moment Johnny Tresano came in with one nickel clutched in his fist. He was so intent on the candies he hardly noticed me. He stood and stood, trying to decide.

"Make up your mind or take yourself off," she growled.

She had gone back behind the counter. I waited for her to look at me again so that I could thank her. But when he left she turned her back and began moving things around on the shelves. I had meant to buy some jujubes but I lost my nerve. After all, everybody knew she hated kids. She was probably sorry now that she'd fixed my knee. I slunk out without once opening my mouth.

Yet, whenever I looked down and saw the Band-Aid, I felt guilty. As soon as one corner came loose, I pulled it off and threw it away. I didn't go near the store for weeks.

— — — — — — — — —

She was terribly fat. She got so hot in summer that her hair hung down in wet strings and her clothes looked limp. In winter she wore the same sweater every day, a man's gray one, too big, with the sleeves pushed up. They kept slipping down and she'd shove them

continues

back a million times a day. Yet she never rolled up the cuffs to make them shorter.

She never took days off. She was always there. We didn't like her or hate her. We sort of knew that selling stuff to kids for a trickle of small change wasn't a job anybody would choose—especially in that poky little place with flies in summer and the door being opened all winter, letting in blasts of cold air. Even after that day when she fixed my knee, I didn't once wonder about her life.

Then I stopped at BUELLS one afternoon and she wasn't there. Instead, a man and woman I'd never laid eyes on were behind the counter sorting through stacks of stuff. They were getting some boxes down off a high shelf right then so they didn't hear me come in. I was so amazed I just stood there gawking.

– – – – – – – – –

"How Ma stood this cruddy hole I'll never know!" the woman said, backing away from a cloud of dust. "Didn't she ever clean?"

"Give the subject a rest, Glo," he answered. "She's dead. She won't bother you any longer."

"I tried, Harry. You know I tried. Over and over, I told her she could move in with us. God knows I could have used a bit of cash and her help looking after those kids."

I think I must have made a sound then. Anyway, she whirled around and saw me.

continues

"This place is closed," she snapped. "Harry, I thought I told you to lock the door. What did you want?"

I didn't want anything from her. But I still could not believe Mrs. Buell wasn't there. I stared around.

"I said we're shut. If you don't want anything, beat it," she told me.

The minute I got home I phoned Emily. She said her mother had just read it in the paper.

"She had a daughter!" Emily said, her voice echoing my own sense of shock. "She died of a heart attack. Kate, her whole name was Katharine Ann Buell."

"Katharine," I said slowly. My name is really Katharine although only Dad calls me by it. "I can't believe it somehow."

"No," Emily said. "She was always just Mrs. Buell."

I told her about Glo and Harry. After we hung up though, I tried to imagine Mrs. Buell as a child. Instead, I saw her bending down putting that Band-Aid on my knee. Her hair had been thin on top, I remembered, and she'd had dandruff. She had tried not to hurt me. Glo's voice, talking about her, had been so cold. Had she had anyone who loved her? It seemed unlikely. Why hadn't I smiled back?

But, to be honest, something else bothered me even more. Her going had left a hole in my life. Because of it I knew, for the first time, that nothing was safe—not even the everyday, taken-for-granted background of my being. Like Mrs. Buell, pushing up her sweater sleeves and giving me my change.

In this story, a girl named Kate tells about Mrs. Buell, a grouchy old lady who owns a store in her neighborhood. One day Kate trips and falls in the store, and Mrs. Buell picks her up and puts a Band-Aid on her knee. Kate is surprised to find out that Mrs. Buell has a nice side. She doesn't think about Mrs. Buell much after that until she goes into the store one day and discovers that Mrs. Buell has died. Kate learns that the old woman had children and a whole other life that Kate knew nothing about. Kate realizes that she never tried to get to know Mrs. Buell. She also realizes that "nothing was safe" in her life. Even the everyday things that she takes for granted can suddenly disappear.

I would recommend this story because it made me think about my own life and how I sometimes overlook people. In the story, Kate didn't pay much attention to Mrs. Buell, and she was sorry about that when the lady died. That made me think about how I need to pay more attention to people in my life and show them that I care about them.

This book is a biography of Jesse Owens, one of the greatest track-and-field stars who ever lived. Jesse grew up in a poor family and was often sick when he was a boy. By junior high school, though, he had developed into a strong athlete. In high school and college, he set records in many track events, including the 220-yard dash and the high jump. In 1936, Jesse became a hero around the world when he won four gold medals at the Olympics in Berlin, Germany. After the Olympics, he made speeches and wrote books about his life and issues facing the black community. He died in 1980.

I would recommend this book. It shows how Jesse Owens overcame poverty and prejudice to become a hero. I especially liked the part where he proved to Hitler at the Olympics that African Americans, Jews, and other minorities are not inferior.

The children were always good during the month of August, especially when it began to get near the twenty-third. It was on this day that Professor Hugo's Interplanetary Zoo settled down for its annual six-hour visit to the Chicago area.

Before daybreak the crowds would form, long lines of children and adults both, each one clutching his or her dollar, and waiting with wonderment to see what race of strange creatures the Professor had brought this year.

In the past they had sometimes been treated to three-legged creatures from Venus, or tall, thin men from Mars, or even snakelike horrors from somewhere more distant. This year, as the great round ship settled slowly to earth in the huge tri-city parking area just outside of Chicago, they watched with awe as the sides slowly slid up to reveal the familiar barred cages. In them were some wild breed of nightmare—small, horselike animals that moved with quick, jerking motions and constantly chattered in a high-pitched tongue. The citizens of Earth clustered around as Professor Hugo's crew quickly collected the waiting dollars, and soon the good Professor himself made an appearance, wearing his many-colored rainbow cape and top hat. "Peoples of Earth," he called into his microphone.

The crowd's noise died down as he continued. "Peoples of Earth, this year you see a real treat for your single dollar—the little-known horse-spider people of Kaan—brought to you across a million miles of space at great expense. Gather around, study them, listen to them, tell your friends about them. But hurry! My ship can remain here only six hours!"

continues

And the crowds slowly filed by, at once horrified and fascinated by these strange creatures that looked like horses but ran up the walls of their cages like spiders. "This is certainly worth a dollar," one man remarked, hurrying away. "I'm going home to get the wife."

All day long it went like that, until ten thousand people had filed by the barred cages set into the side of the spaceship. Then, as the six-hour limit ran out, Professor Hugo once more took microphone in hand. "We must go now, but we will return next year on this date. And if you enjoyed our zoo this year, phone your friends in other cities about it. We will land in New York tomorrow, and next week on to London, Paris, Rome, Hong Kong, and Tokyo. Then on to other worlds!"

He waved farewell to them, and as the ship rose from the ground the Earth peoples agreed that this had been the very best Zoo yet....

— — — — — — — — — —

Some two months and three planets later, the silver ship of Professor Hugo settled at last onto the familiar jagged rocks of Kaan, and the queer horse-spider creatures filed quickly out of their cages. Professor Hugo was there to say a few parting words, and then they scurried away in a hundred different directions, seeking their homes among the rocks.

In one, the she-creature was happy to see the return of her mate and offspring. She babbled a greeting in the strange tongue and hurried to embrace them. "It was a long time you were gone! Was it good?"

continues

And the he-creature nodded. "The little one enjoyed it especially. We visited eight worlds and saw many things."

The little one ran up the wall of the cave. "On the place called Earth it was the best. The creatures there wear garments over their skins, and they walk on two legs."

"But isn't it dangerous?" asked the she-creature.

"No," her mate answered. "There are bars to protect us from them. We remain right in the ship. Next time you must come with us. It is well worth the nineteen commocs it costs."

And the little one nodded. "It was the very best Zoo ever...."

_____
_____
_____
_____
_____
_____
_____
_____
_____
_____
_____
_____
_____
_____
_____
_____
_____
_____
_____

An icy blast roared through the Skyvan transport plane as the rear door opened to the bright blue sky. On an April morning in 1991, above the flat fields of Cambridgeshire, England, three skydivers were about to make a parachute jump they would never forget.

Richard Maynard was making his first jump. He had paid a substantial fee to plummet from 3,600m (12,000ft), strapped to Mike Smith, a skilled parachute instructor. Expecting this experience (known as a "tandem jump") to be the thrill of a lifetime, Maynard had also commissioned instructor Ronnie O'Brien, to videotape him.

O'Brien leaped backwards from the plane to film Maynard and Smith's exit. The pair plunged down after him, speeding up to 290kmph (180mph) in the first 15 seconds. They soon overtook O'Brien, and Smith released a small drogue parachute to slow them down to a speed where it would be safe to open his main parachute, without it giving them a backbreaking jolt. But here disaster struck. As the chute flew from its container, the cord holding it became entangled around Smith's neck. It pulled tight, strangling him, and he quickly lost consciousness.

Watching from 90m (300ft) above, O'Brien saw the two men spinning out of control, and when the drogue parachute failed to open he knew something had gone terribly wrong. Both men were just 45 seconds from the ground. If O'Brien could not help them, they both faced certain death.

O'Brien changed from the usual spread-eagled posture of a skydiver, and swooped down through the air toward the plummeting pair, with his legs pressed tightly together and arms by his side. He

continues

How it all happened

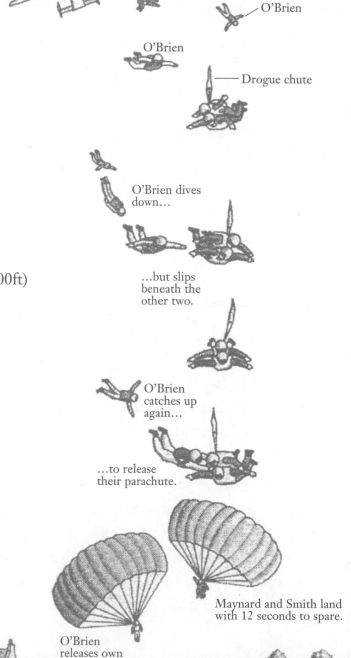

3,600m (12,000ft)
O'Brien jumps from aircraft, followed immediately by Maynard and Smith.

Maynard and Smith

O'Brien

O'Brien

3,000m (10,000ft)
Smith deploys drogue chute which becomes tangled around his neck.

Drogue chute

2,300m (7,500ft)
Smith loses consciousness. O'Brien dives down to help.

O'Brien dives down…

2,500–1,500m (7,000–5,000ft)
O'Brien catches up with tandem divers but slips underneath them
(25 seconds to impact).

…but slips beneath the other two.

O'Brien catches up again…

900m (3,000ft)
O'Brien catches up again.

700m (2,500ft)
Parachute released
(12 seconds to impact).
Smith recovers.

…to release their parachute.

650m (2,250ft)
O'Brien deploys own parachute.

Maynard and Smith land with 12 seconds to spare.

O'Brien releases own parachute.

had to judge his descent very carefully. If he overshot, he would have little chance of saving the two men, but this veteran of 2,000 jumps knew what he was doing.

Positioning himself right in front of them, he quickly realized what had happened, and tried to grab hold of Smith so he could release his main parachute. But diving at the same speed was extremely difficult. O'Brien would be within arms length of the falling men and then lurch out of reach. Then suddenly, he fell way below them.

Time was fast running out. The ground was a mere 20 seconds away and O'Brien knew he had only one more chance to save their lives. He spread his arms and legs out to slow his descent, and this time managed to connect with the pair. Whirling around and around, O'Brien searched frantically for the handle that would release Smith's parachute.

With barely 12 seconds before they hit the ground, O'Brien found the handle, and the large main chute billowed out above them. Slowed by the chute, Smith and Maynard shot away as O'Brien continued to plunge down. He released his own parachute when he was safely out of the way, a few seconds before he himself would have hit the ground.

By the time the tandem pair had landed, Smith had recovered consciousness, but collapsed almost immediately. Only then did Maynard realize something had gone wrong. Caught up in the excitement of the jump, with adrenaline coursing through his body and the wind roaring in his ears, he had had no idea that anything out of the ordinary had happened.

Name: _____

My Opinions About

Evidence

Opinions

Article
from timeforkids.com (May 15, 2001) by Dina Maasarani

Is Dodge Ball Too Dangerous?

Many schools are banning a gym game they say is too violent

Is dodge ball on the verge of being tossed out? Dodge ball, one of the most popular games in gym class, is now also being called one of the most dangerous. More and more schools are banning dodge ball, a game in which kids throw balls at other kids who have to avoid—or dodge—them. Now, the game itself is having to dodge some pretty serious criticism.

Why Ban Dodge Ball?

What's all the fuss about a game that's been played across the country for decades? School districts in states such as Texas, Virginia, Maine and Massachusetts have banned it because many educators and parents say dodge ball is a violent and aggressive game. They say a game where there is a "human target" makes it more likely for kids to get hurt.

Neil Williams, an Eastern Connecticut State University physical education professor, has created a Physical Education Hall of Shame. He considers dodge ball (also known as bombardment, burning ball, killer ball, prison ball, and ball chaser) the most shameful school sport on his list. "It allows the stronger kids to pick on and target the weaker kids," Williams says. Critics also complain the game is not a good form of exercise because it requires kids who are eliminated (or hit by the ball) to sit on the sidelines while others get to keep

continues

playing. "If a boy doesn't throw hard and make a hit, the other boys call him a girl," says Lilla Atherton, a fifth grader in Fairfax County, Virginia, where the game has been banned.

Dodge Ball Defenders

Fans of the classic game say it's simple and fun and helps kids improve their reflexes and hand-eye coordination. Dodge ball supporters also say injuries are rare because most gym teachers do not allow students to aim for the head and because most balls are made from foam or other soft materials. Martha Kupferschmidt, an official at the Murray school district in Utah, wonders why dodge ball is being singled out when other sports like football, kickball and wrestling are also aggressive. "If we are going to ban dodge ball for aggressiveness, we would have to look at a whole gamut of sports," she says.

While some adults are debating whether kids should be playing dodge ball, others are starting to play the game themselves. The first-ever world dodge ball indoor championship for adults was held in Schaumburg, Illinois in January. "Dodge Ball Day 2001" is scheduled for July 28, also in Illinois.

Changing the Rules of the Game

Some school districts that do not want to ban dodge ball have instead decided to change the rules to make it less violent. In several districts, kids who are hit with the ball get to re-enter the game so there are no hurt feelings. In other schools, kids aim at a deflated ball instead of other kids.

Turn It Off!
Next week, millions of people will go TV-free. How about you?

On April 22, millions of TVs around the world will go blank. But instead of fiddling with the remote or calling the cable company, avid TV watchers everywhere will take drastic action. Entire families will go outside to ride bikes; groups of friends will play games. Will you join in—or will you just sit there and watch?

April 22–28 is TV-Turnoff Week. TV-Turnoff Network, a nonprofit organization, has promoted the annual event since 1995. In the beginning, only a few thousand people took part. This year, there will be participants in every state and more than 12 countries.

TV's Many Turnoffs

Each year, kids in the U.S. spend more time glued to the tube than doing anything else—except for sleeping! People have worried about the effects of TV ever since the 1940s, when television became popular. Over the years, health care groups like the American Academy of Pediatrics and the American Medical Association have voiced their concern. They point to studies that link excessive TV viewing to such problems as bad eating habits, lack of exercise, obesity and violent behavior.

Two weeks ago, a new study published in the journal *Science* gave fresh evidence of a connection between TV viewing and violence. Psychologist Jeffrey G. Johnson and his research team followed

continues

children in 707 families for 17 years. The researchers found that kids who watched more than one hour of TV a day were more likely than other kids to take part in aggressive and violent behavior as they grew older. Says Johnson, the link between TV, with all its violent shows, and aggressive behavior "has gotten to the point where it's overwhelming."

Others worry about the impact of commercials on kids. One study found that during four hours of Saturday-morning cartoons, TV networks ran 202 ads for junk foods. The steady stream of reminders to buy sugary soda, cereal and candy are one reason that more than one in eight American kids is overweight. Long hours sitting in front of the tube are another reason. "Almost anything uses more energy than watching TV," says Dr. William H. Dietz of the U.S. Centers for Disease Control and Prevention in Atlanta, Georgia.

Enjoying Life, Unplugged

TV-Turnoff Network wants to encourage life outside the box. "We're not anti-TV," says the group's director, Frank Vespe. The goal is to help kids tune into real life so that "they won't have time for TV."

But this is an adult speaking. Is it really possible to live without popular TV show? Sarah Foote, of Burke, Virginia, says she made it through TV-Turnoff Week last year—and enjoyed herself! After a few days, says Sarah, 10, "I thought, 'Why did I ever need TV?'" Her brother Nathaniel, 8, agrees: "There are about 8,000 other things you can do."

continues

Still, some kids can't picture life without TV. Christian Cardenas, 10, of New York City, doesn't plan on tuning out. "It entertains you on rainy days," he says.

Could you go without TV for a whole week? Says TV-Turnoff veteran Carly Cara, 11, of Niles, Illinois: "You're doing so many fun things that before you know it, it's over!"

Name: _____

List the books that you would like to read this summer.
Write the author's name and a few words to remind you what the book is about.

Book	Author	Reminder

The Legend of Sleepy Hollow
by Washington Irving

Ichabod Crane has just arrived to Sleepy Hollow and has met a lot of people. Those people have told Ichabod the legend of Sleepy Hollow.

This legend is about a headless horseman who goes around cutting other people's heads in search of his own. This legend scared Ichabod every time it was told. Ichabod Crane had fallen in love with Katrina, a very rich girl, a couple of weeks after he arrived to Sleepy Hollow. One day Ichabod was invited to Katrina's party, and before the party was over a woman started to say the legend of Sleepy Hollow and at the end she said the only way you can escape the headless horseman is by crossing the bridge. That night Ichabod and his horse ran as fast as they could to reach their house. Finally he was up to the bridge that meant that he was near his house. Then something got in his way, it was the headless horseman. Did Ichabod ever escape?

I think that this book was very interesting because it was a legend about a headless horseman that lost his head in a war and since then has been looking for it by cutting other people's heads off. I recommend this book to people who like scary legends that took place a long time ago.

This story reminds me of 'Bloody Mary' because they are both scary and they are both legends. What makes this story more scary is that it has been told for more than 100 years and it has been told by people who are already dead.

Name:

Things to Include in My Book Review

Book Title:

Thoughts About My Reading Life

Name: _____

What are some of your favorite kinds of books now? Why?

_____

_____

_____

Where is your favorite place to read?

_____

_____

_____

What does the word *reading* mean to you?

_____

_____

_____

When you don't understand something you are reading, what do you do?

_____

_____

_____

What kinds of books did you read for the first time this year? What topics did you read about for the first time?

_____

_____

_____

Name:
_____

How have you grown in your ability to work with a partner this year?

_____

_____

_____

_____

_____

How have we done at becoming a caring and safe community this year? What makes you think so?

_____

_____

_____

_____

_____

How has being part of this community helped you this year?

_____

_____

_____

_____

_____

IDR Journal

Reading Log

Name: _____

Date	Title	Author
comment:		
comment:		
comment:		
comment:		
comment:		
comment:		

Reading Log

Date	Title	Author
comment:		
comment:		
comment:		
comment:		
comment:		
comment:		
comment:		

Reading Log

Name: _____

Date	Title	Author
comment:		
comment:		
comment:		
comment:		
comment:		
comment:		
comment:		

Name:

Reading Log

Date	Title	Author

comment:

| | | |

comment:

| | | |

comment:

| | | |

comment:

| | | |

comment:

| | | |

comment:

| | | |

comment:

Reading Log

Name: _____

Date	Title	Author

comment:

comment:

comment:

comment:

comment:

comment:

comment:

Name:

Date	Title	Author
comment:		
comment:		
comment:		
comment:		
comment:		
comment:		
comment:		

Name: _____ Date: _____

Name: _____ Date: _____

Name: _____ Date: _____

Name: _____ Date: _____

Name: _____ Date: _____

Name: _____ Date: _____

Name: _____   Date: _____

_____

_____

_____

_____

_____

_____

_____

_____

_____

_____

_____

_____

_____

_____

_____

_____

_____

_____

_____

_____

_____

Name: _____ Date: _____

Name: _____ Date: _____

_____

_____

_____

_____

_____

_____

_____

_____

_____

_____

_____

_____

_____

_____

_____

_____

_____

_____

Name: _____   Date: _____

_____

_____

_____

_____

_____

_____

_____

_____

_____

_____

_____

_____

_____

_____

_____

_____

_____

_____

Name: _____   Date: _____

Name: _____   Date: _____

Name: _____ Date: _____

_____

_____

_____

_____

_____

_____

_____

_____

_____

_____

_____

_____

_____

_____

_____

_____

_____

_____

_____

_____

_____

_____

Name: _____ Date: _____

Name: _____ Date: _____

_____
_____
_____
_____
_____
_____
_____
_____
_____
_____
_____
_____
_____
_____
_____
_____
_____
_____

Name: _____ Date: _____

Name: _____   Date: _____

_____

_____

_____

_____

_____

_____

_____

_____

_____

_____

_____

_____

_____

_____

_____

_____

_____

_____

_____

_____

_____

_____

_____

_____

_____

Name: _____ Date: _____

Name:

Date:

Name: _____ Date: _____

Name: _____ Date: _____

_____

_____

_____

_____

_____

_____

_____

_____

_____

_____

_____

_____

_____

_____

_____

_____

_____

_____

_____

_____

_____

_____

Name: _____   Date: _____

_____

_____

_____

_____

_____

_____

_____

_____

_____

_____

_____

_____

_____

_____

_____

_____

_____

_____

_____

_____

_____

_____

Name: _____ Date: _____

Name: _____ Date: _____

Name: _____ Date: _____

_____

_____

_____

_____

_____

_____

_____

_____

_____

_____

_____

_____

_____

_____

_____

_____

_____

_____

_____

_____

_____

Name: _____   Date: _____

Name: _____ Date: _____

Name: _____ Date: _____

Name: _____   Date: _____

Name: _____   Date: _____

Name: _____   Date: _____

Name: _____   Date: _____

Name: _____ Date: _____

Name: _____ Date: _____

_____

_____

_____

_____

_____

_____

_____

_____

_____

_____

_____

_____

_____

_____

_____

_____

_____

_____

_____

_____

_____

Name: _____ Date: _____

Name: _____ Date: _____

Name: _____   Date: _____